MONEY MANAGEMENT & ENTREPRENEURS

Making Money Work For You

Dr. Sheika Square

LIFE & BUSINESS COACH

Priority Writing Approach
2000 Louisiana
#751035
New Orleans, LA 70175

www.drsheikasquare.com

Copy editor: Lynel Johnson Washington

ISBN-13: 978-0-9986290-8-7

CONTENTS

Where there was once lack, there will be abundance.

Dr. Sheika Square

Introduction

Having big plans for your life means having even bigger plans for your money. However, so many people settle for less; feeling that the price is too high or the dream is unattainable. If you consider yourself to be "broke" right now, your mind has the illness, not your wallet. If you are willing to shift your habits around money and your beliefs around the importance and purpose of money, you can have more money to manage. When you learned how to count as a child you learned how to have money then as well. I am ready to start the discussion and will assume that you have $1, so let's start there…

1

Become the Master of Your Money: Create Money Goals

As a person in business and as a person aspiring to be at the top of your field, you must learn how to create goals for your money. Goals have allowed me to get from point A to point B and goals have allowed me to skip steps. Mastering your life comes with creating a roadmap for what you want to accomplish, how you want to accomplish it, and when you must have it accomplished. Without goals you become a master of nothing, wandering around aimlessly, hoping for the best.

Creating money goals dictates the amount of money that will be reinvested/invested into your business to grow the business and allotted for you to live the type of life you want to live. What type of entrepreneur you are or what type of entrepreneur you are aspiring to be also determines the money goals you must create. If you are looking to grow your business, you need to understand what costs are associated with that growth. You could hope for the best and you may grow, even make some money. However, it is unlikely that you will experience the exact success you intended inside of your life and business without clear direction.

Step 1 of Mastering Your Money: Create a goal that outlines how much money you need to bring your business to the next level or start a new business. You can do this by writing out the supplies and expenses you expect to acquire or need within a certain timeframe. Then allocate dollar amounts to each item. Total up the amount and add in your salary and the money you will need to bring on employees and/or consultants.

Step 2 of Mastering Your Money: Understand your why when planning out your goals. Your why is a key step in mastering your money and creating the wealth that you desire inside of your business. Understand why you want it. This is often overlooked and underutilized. Clarify why you want this type of wealth accumulation in your life and in your business. Become very clear on your desired outcome and the impact it will have on your quality of life. This is what will sustain you when you feel like giving up.

Step 3 of Mastering Your Money: When? When do you want to accomplish this goal or when do you want to have this money in place?

For instance, let's say your goal is, "I want to make $30,000 a month, every month." You would write out, "I make $30,000 every 30 days for the rest of this decade/year/the time that I am in business." This allows you to put in perspective how much you want to accumulate and by when.

Step 4 of Mastering Your Money: Have both products and services and understand their earning ability. Decide how much money you can sell a product for and then how many of those products you would need to sell to meet your goal. For my business, I offer books, courses, consultations, business coaching, etc.… When I want to increase my income, I look across my products and services and create a plan. This plan includes marketing to sell a certain number of products of a certain title and services at cost.

Step 5 of Mastering Your Money: Get to work. Notice I did not say pray and sit down. You must act. Get busy doing what you need to do to have what you want to have.

My Top 5 Money Goals
JANUARY

My Top 5 Money Goals
FEBRUARY

My Top 5 Money Goals
MARCH

My Top 5 Money Goals
APRIL

My Top 5 Money Goals
MAY

My Top 5 Money Goals
JUNE

My Top 5 Money Goals
JULY

My Top 5 Money Goals
AUGUST

My Top 5 Money Goals
SEPTEMBER

My Top 5 Money Goals
OCTOBER

My Top 5 Money Goals
NOVEMBER

My Top 5 Money Goals
DECEMBER

WORKING TOWARDS SMART GOALS

A mind map is a diagram used to visuallyorganize information. A mind map is hierarchical and shows relationships among pieces of the whole

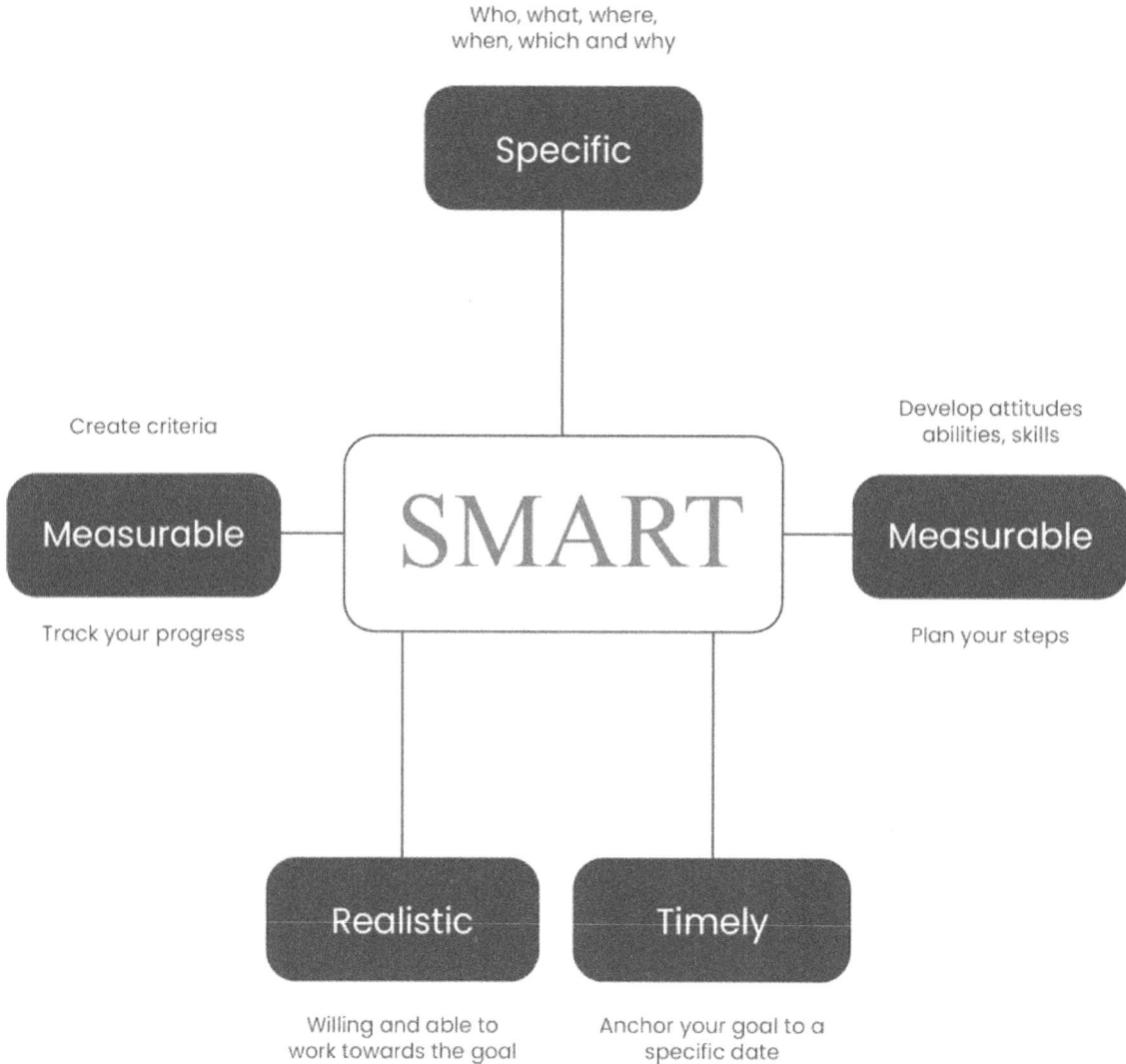

Who, what, where, when, which and why

Specific

Create criteria

Develop attitudes abilities, skills

Measurable

SMART

Measurable

Track your progress

Plan your steps

Realistic

Timely

Willing and able to work towards the goal

Anchor your goal to a specific date

Products & Services

PRODUCTS   **SERVICES**

Products & Services

PRODUCTS   SERVICES

NOTES

NOTES

NOTES

NOTES

NOTES

2

Track Your Expenses

Tracking those expenses!!! Everything that I talk about in this book is important. However, I get extremely excited when I start to discuss the actual dollar. For the sake of clarity, still, note that tracking your expenses is different from outlining your money goals or analyzing your business' financial standing with products and services. Tracking your expenses is about understanding how much is coming in versus how much you are putting out. How much you have in savings, that is allocated to the business, and how much of that money is being used on business expenses. We are talking allocation versus spending and in many cases, money that is not allocated but is being spent.

As an entrepreneur, whether in the early stages or the multi-million dollar stage, having a wealth of knowledge and the ability to analyze your profit and loss statements, even after your accountant does it, will save you in taxes, ward off theft, and keep you ahead in your field. The simplest way to track is to compare total money spent versus money made. If you receive $2,000 in deposits from products and/or services but you spend $4,000, tracking allows you to see what is being spent and that you are overspending as it relates to revenue.

Another way to track expenses is to look at itemized bank statements and note where your money goes each month. For this you can use apps, bookkeeping software, or your bank's website. I like to track my expenses in a notebook or in The Affirmation Journal (the one I use is on drsheikasquare.com). I find that tracking my expenses by hand keeps me mindful of my abundance.

Why Track?

Years ago, when I was broke, I adopted the ideology that since no money was coming in there was no need to track my expenses. The entire time I had that mindset I was broke. Then I started to manage every dollar and cent that came into my household and how it was spent, down to the penny. I noticed I started to have more money to manage. As I managed, my money grew. As my money grew, I kept tracking my expenses. Any book you read on money, wealth creation, or wealth manifestation will tell you that in order to make more money and have more money, you must be mindful of what you already have. Now that I have more money, I may not calculate every penny, but I do still track and monitor my profits and my spending.

Expense Tracker Worksheet

Date	Expense	Amount	Category	Notes

Expense Tracker Worksheet

Date	Expense	Amount	Category	Notes

Savings Calculator

Week	Deposit	Balance	Week	Deposit	Balance
1	$1	$1	27	$27	$378
2	$2	$3	28	$28	$406
3	$3	$6	29	$29	$435
4	$4	$10	30	$30	$465
5	$5	$15	31	$31	$496
6	$6	$21	32	$32	$528
7	$7	$28	33	$33	$561
8	$8	$36	34	$34	$595
9	$9	$45	35	$35	$630
10	$10	$55	36	$36	$666
11	$11	$66	37	$37	$703
12	$12	$78	38	$38	$741
13	$13	$91	39	$39	$780
14	$14	$105	40	$40	$820
15	$15	$120	41	$41	$861
16	$16	$136	42	$42	$903
17	$17	$153	43	$43	$946
18	$18	$171	44	$44	$990
19	$19	$190	45	$45	$1,035
20	$20	$210	46	$46	$1,081
21	$21	$231	47	$47	$1,128
22	$22	$253	48	$48	$1,176
23	$23	$276	49	$49	$1,225
24	$24	$300	50	$50	$1,275
25	$25	$325	51	$51	$1,326
26	$26	$351	52	$52	$1,378

NOTES

NOTES

NOTES

NOTES

NOTES

3

Have Separate Accounts

Have separate accounts!!! You can create legal issues for yourself if you do not separate your money. It also becomes much harder to track your expenses for your business, and for your household, if you do not have the right accounts in place. It is not expensive to open new accounts and in many instances, it is free. Many banks will offer promotions to business owners and pay them money just to bank with their bank.

Once you are set up legally as a business or once you have plans to structure your business legally, you must consider separate accounts. A personal account and a business account for your money makes economic sense and offers minimum protection of your funds against lawsuits, audits, and commingling accusations. It is also a good money habit to organize and separate your money. Additionally, the number of accounts you need will grow as you grow and the types of accounts you require will shift with your needs. Consider adding at least one small bank and/or credit union to your financial portfolio. These institutions have been cited for favorable lending practices as a result of their ability to create relationships with their customers. However, a personal account, a business account for every business, and a merchant account connected to your online shop will get you started and financially positioned even as a seasoned entrepreneur.

Merchant Accounts

Choose your merchant account based on your requirements as a business owner and the number of transactions you expect to complete each month. Types of merchant accounts include PayPal®, Stripe, Square Capital, and many others.

Pro Tip

It is especially important to make sure that your business documents are in order prior to creating a business account or merchant account. Once you have chosen a bank, they will ask for your business articles and other legal documents. The bank will also verify these documents before activating your account, lending to you or your business, and prior to linking merchant accounts to your primary account.

✓ Account Set-Up Checklist

Documents Needed To Set Up A Business Account

- [ ] Secure your EIN
- [ ] Obtain your Secretary of State Credentials
- [ ] Have an ID/Passport
- [ ] Your Social Security Card and/or Birth Certificate
- [ ] Business Address
- [ ]
- [ ]
- [ ]
- [ ]
- [ ]
- [ ]
- [ ]
- [ ]

NOTES

NOTES

NOTES

NOTES

NOTES

4

Put Yourself on an Allowance

First, let me begin by saying that there are various schools of thought on this topic. Many multi-millionaires believe that you limit your growth potential when you move in scarcity; i.e. putting limits on your money. However, an allowance has very little to do with being able to afford or not afford something. When starting out, an allowance helps you to manage a limited amount of money. Putting an allowance in place also helps you to become aware of your spending. If you are building your business and you are putting a lot of money behind your products, behind your branding, and paying consultants, an allowance can add an extra layer to managing your money.

When I started paying myself an allowance, my allowance was $50 a week. Then it grew to $150 and then $300 and so on… Now I have more money than bills and more disposable income. Nevertheless, I still utilize an allowance, because I like to know how much I am spending while spending it. An allowance has proven beneficial for many of my clients as well. When learning the power of your thoughts and beliefs as it relates to money, having an allowance can allow you to ease into accepting abundance. It can also help on the journey of learning new and effective money habits.

Whether you are a multi-million-dollar earner or thousandaire (yes I made that up), learning to manage and control your spending allows more space for growth and better utilization of what funds are available. Pick a system, cash allowance or electronic allocation, that works for you and get busy making the money.

Monthly Income Worksheet

Account	Date	Description	Category	Money IN	Money OUT	Balance

NOTES

NOTES

NOTES

NOTES

NOTES

5

Set Time to Examine All of Your Money

If you have ever had a boyfriend or girlfriend (yes, I am going there), then you know in the beginning you spend a lot of time with that person. The same should be true for your money. In order to make any relationship grow, whether it is a friendship, family relationship, romantic relationship, or the relationship you have with your money, there must be a time investment. Spending time with your money helps you to gain perspective, it makes tracking insightful, and it helps you understand if you are hitting the goals that you have set for your products, services, and team. Spending time with your money helps you to resolve any of the financial needs of your business as well. You also uncover what money needs to be put where when you spend time with your finances.

As you gain momentum in your business and invest more time in analyzing your profits, you start to also realize that certain products and services do better than others. You realize what accounts are linked to services that produce a better bottom line. You notice merchant accounts that seem to constantly produce revenue from the part of your ad sales with high conversion rates. You realize that customers buy a lot of books and you put more money behind courses because that area of your business performs better than any other area. Knowing when to do this and why comes from spending time with your money.

Nevertheless, the frequency at which you choose to do this analysis depends on two factors, the amount of income coming in and the amount of expenses paid (what you discover when you track your spending). Although, when you analyze your money you also track your income and budget, your spending analysis dissects what marketing is working, what consultants you should keep paying, and what did not work well at all. Spending time with your money helps you to gain perspective on your spending and allows you to get better acquainted with your money.

What's Coming In VS. What's Going Out

Coming In   Going Out

NOTES

NOTES

NOTES

NOTES

NOTES

6

Priority Notifications: Turn off Distractions and Turn on Money Alerts

Every area of your life should depict what you truly believe about your life, your money and your business. The social media brands you engage with, the apps that have access to you, and the countless hours you spend swiping and scrolling all speak to (and determine) what you believe about wealth (how much wealth you possess). Having an overwhelming number of alerts, that don't matter, pouring into your devices from random sources will keep you broke. The social media influencers, people and brands that you follow should raise your energy and grow your level of consciousness. For the brands and people that do not, intentionally leave the notifications off.

Having certain notifications post singularly to your phone, mobile device or tablet will help you to focus on your money and keep you tuned in to all-things money. Conversely, a plethora of notifications can overwhelm your senses and dull your ability to make decisions. Over time it can deplete your energy and diminish your capacity for zoning in on priority items related to making money. In making the decision between notifications or no notifications, focus in on the ones that matter.

What Notifications Matter?

Text messages from very important people and those about business can support your goals and allow for much-needed social interaction. Website notifications, when people subscribe, buy products, and schedule consultations/services, are priority and when scheduled correctly, can help with analyzing your business. I personally like to know when people schedule appointments, even though I have assistants and specialists for that. Notifications that allow you to see when you are making money, whether it is from product sales, services, stock investments, etc... are also great to have turned on and showing as a banner alert on your phone. However, I like email notifications (these do not come to my phone) for my credit, stock buys, and business growth & funding opportunities.

Where's My Attention

IMPORTANT NOTIFICATION	UNIMPORTANT NOTIFICATIONS

NOTES

NOTES

NOTES

NOTES

NOTES

7

Who Are You Letting Influence You

We let others influence our mindset, our finances, our relationships and our eating. We constantly have things pouring in from the television, our computers and smart devices, our family, friends, and even random people walking on the street. People from all over the world are attempting to influence you to do things the way they feel they should be done. Therefore, it is important to filter who (what) is influencing your money.

Who are you following? When I open social media, I am inundated with positive energy and quality financial advice. I allow people who will pour into me to influence me. It must be something that grows and edifies for me to let it impact me. Whether you believe it or not, what you are allowing into you will shape your progress for the future and accounts for how much money you are making. There is a saying that "Your circle determines your income." Understand fully that the money in your bank account is directly correlated with who you spend the most time with.

The people you are around and the environment you spend time in, determines how successful you are today. The right network can allow you to skip steps. Although, there is a certain level of push and motivation that you can give yourself, having positive influence around money and abundance can change your circumstance and your life. If you are focusing on growing your money, everything that's pouring in should be on money habits, except as it pertains to self-care. All the people you spend time with should be people who understand the money game, people who are investing, people who are networking and people who are growing businesses. This is how you stay in a constant state of growth.

According to Joseph Murphy, poverty is an illness of the mind. There are many physical and societal reasons why people do not attain high degrees of wealth. However, a pollution of the mind causes an inability to reverse the effects of these poverty-inducing processes. Remaining mindful of what causes peace and growth around life and money will bring more wealth and longevity. Understanding what brings positivity to the mind will also increase your net worth.

Additionally, learn to spend time with masters—people who understand the concept of gaining money and having peace simultaneously. Learn the practice of meditation. Meditation plays a role in how you are influencing yourself. As I sat writing this book, I had a painter come in and out, I stopped to order groceries then cook dinner, the grass-cutter came to get paid and my aunt stopped by. There was a moment where I felt overwhelmed and a bit frazzled. However, I have created habits that have allowed me to center myself and focus on what needs to be focused on. I have learned not to dwell on the negative thoughts that distract me. Abundance is not just financial increase to the detriment of your health. Great wealth can come with great abundance. The who and the what influencing you, however, greatly impacts how quickly you grow wealth and if you attain financial freedom at all.

LET'S GET THINGS DONE TODAY!

Meals:

Breakfast

Lunch

Dinner

Words to live by

Notes

Priorties:

Appointments:

To do:

Water

Clean the house

Things to buy

Monthly Planner

Monday

Priorties/Urgent:

Tuesday

Wednesday

Appointments:

Thursday

Notes:

Friday

Monthly Planner

Monday

Priorties/Urgent:

Tuesday

Wednesday

Appointments:

Thursday

Notes:

Friday

Monthly Planner

Monday

Priorties/Urgent:

Tuesday

Wednesday

Appointments:

Thursday

Notes:

Friday

Monthly Planner

Monday

Priorties/Urgent:

Tuesday

Wednesday

Appointments:

Thursday

Notes:

Friday

Monthly Planner

Monday

Priorties/Urgent:

Tuesday

Wednesday

Appointments:

Thursday

Notes:

Friday

NOTES

NOTES

NOTES

NOTES

NOTES

8

Clean Up Your Finances

If you are bringing a lot of money in but you are mismanaging it, something or someone can come in and take all of your money. This can happen through a tax audit, paying too much in taxes/interest, or a balancing/bookkeeping error. It is important to keep your money in an honored state. To keep your money in an honored state, you must keep your finances clean. Your taxes should be up to date. Your credit should be good to great or at least acknowledged and improving. There is no bill that you should not be aware of. All of your business finances and business dealings should be under an EIN and processed through a business bank account. To move from surviving to wealth, you must manage your funds and keep them clean.

Credit

No matter how much money you acquire, there is going to be a time when using credit benefits you. Even if you are liquid, a deal can come in and deplete your cash reserves. The benefits of financing a deal outweigh a deal that is done primarily in cash. As you grow financially and/or in business, you are going to want different things. This variation comes with a cost.

Credit that is kept in good condition can allow you to grow your business, start a new business, or even maintain a business that is transitioning. Whatever the situation, you will need good credit and benefit from the use of this good credit.

Some of the things that can impact your credit score negatively are late payments, collection accounts, credit fraud, high balances, not paying business bills as soon as you get them, etc.… A negative score or a lower score will decrease the likelihood of receiving funding from banks and other lending institutions. Conversely, business credit (credit associated with an EIN versus a SSN) allows you to purchase things for your business that cash cannot. You can build business credit by purchasing from different merchants or vendors that report your activity to the credit bureaus. This forces you to be mindful of how you are doing business and handling your finances as well.

Taxes

The fears of not being able to purchase a home, possibly going to jail, or even having all their assets taken, plague many individuals. One of the calls that I get frequently inside of the tax business is, "I have not filed my taxes in many years." What usually also follows is, "And now I'm not sleeping at night." The financial remedy is to have clean finances and part of that is filing your taxes.

Receiving a letter in the mail from the Internal Revenue Service (IRS) and throwing it away only furthers your fears and accrues more interest. Even if it is a little scary, make sure your taxes are in order, filed and paid. As a tax business owner, I can attest to confronting IRS debt versus ignoring it. When it pertains to taxes, as is true for credit, the benefits of paying any debt over time outweighs having to pay all of it at once, even if there is interest involved, and especially as it relates to your tax bill.

Credit and up-to-date taxes allow you to leverage other people's money. That is the secret of wealth, building faster, and staying liquid. To move into wealth, you must stop ignoring and start managing. Building a lucrative business requires clean finances. Clean finances requires management, strategy, analyzing and tracking.

365 Days Business Checklist

Number 1 on my list:

Things I want that don't matter:

Things I need:

How much cash I have:

How much cash I need:

Credit I have access to:

Tax Prep Readiness Questionaire

Use these questions to assess your readiness throughout tax season or together before you head to your local tax office. For specific questions and to schedule a consultation, call Square Tax Group at (504) 517-5581.

Whats is your occupation?

Did you and your dependents have health insurance the whole year? If not, please specify which months you had insurance.

Was your insurance through your job, marketplace, Medicaid, or Medicare?

Are you or any of your dependents disabled? Please specifty.

Do you have a vehicle used for work?

What is the make and model of vehicle?

Tax Prep Readiness Questionaire

Use these questions to assess your readiness throughout tax season or together before you head to your local tax office. For specific questions and to schedule a consultation, call Square Tax Group at (504) 517-5581.

How much did you pay for the vehicle?

Date placed in service.

How many business miles?

Total mileage?

Gas for the year?

Oil changes for the year?

Tax Prep Readiness Questionaire

Use these questions to assess your readiness throughout tax season or together before you head to your local tax office. For specific questions and to schedule a consultation, call Square Tax Group at (504) 517-5581.

Repairs?

Maintenance?

Tires?

Garage?

Insurance?

Parking fees and tolls?

Business meals?

Tax Prep Readiness Questionaire

Use these questions to assess your readiness throughout tax season or together before you head to your local tax office. For specific questions and to schedule a consultation, call Square Tax Group at (504) 517-5581.

Business entertainment?

Business Advertising?

Business expenses?

Do you have a dependent that attended grade school? Please provide the name of the school and any expenses such as, book expenses tuition, supplies, uniforms, and transportation sercice.

Tax Prep Readiness Questionaire

Use these questions to assess your readiness throughout tax season or together before you head to your local tax office. For specific questions and to schedule a consultation, call Square Tax Group at (504) 517-5581.

Did you pay childcare expenses? If so, how much did you pay for the year, the name of the facility or person, address, EIN number or SSN if it's a person.

Did your dependents live with you 12 montha? if not how many months.

Did you and your dependents have health insurance?

Please provide social security cards and birth certificate.

NOTES

NOTES

NOTES

NOTES

NOTES

9

Reinvest

Traveling and the finer things in life are wonderful; however, make sure you are putting a percentage of the money you earn back into your business. Commit to a percentage of revenue that is forwarded directly back into your business. This allows your money and your business to grow faster and more efficiently. Reinvesting into your business helps with scaling, income growth and employee retention. After taking the steps to track your expenses and analyze your business (through principles mentioned in the above chapters), focus on where a financial reinvestment would be most beneficial.

Priority Pieces

Understanding your money will allow you to recognize where to put more money. I am currently the CEO of two businesses that I started, a business and life-coaching firm (dba Dr. Sheika Square) and Square Tax Group (dba Square and McGary Tax Services in 2019 and 2020). Inside of the business/life-coaching firm, I help people with mindset, living their best lives and making more money. With the tax group, we focus on business taxes, bookkeeping and financial planning. In recent years, I have spent thousands of dollars on marketing and branding for the life-coaching firm.

The tax group has gotten more of my strategic planning initiatives. However, I am fully aware of the fact that if I were to pour more time and resources (financial and otherwise) into the tax group it would be HUGE! Although I am planning to do this in upcoming years, my awareness around the need for additional financial reinvestment comes from my time analyzing, tracking and managing my businesses (and their monies).

When you reinvest into your financial growth and/or the financial growth of your business(es), you pour into priority pieces. Growing revenue comes when you put more money behind products and services that are destined to grow by 10%, 48% or 89% with the additional financial backing. Using money to reinvest in your business, and to invest in your business' future, helps to grow your investment. Hiring a coach, creating more coursework, attending conferences/webinars, buying books, etc. are all ways to invest in your business and will prove lucrative over time. If you are a product-based business, additional machinery might be the investment. For my businesses, I have purchased office equipment, websites, marketing and courses. I have also paid for coaches, employees and specific experts. I have seen the greatest return on investment when the purchase helped to grow my intellectual property and tangible goods.

Hiring Help

Hiring help, as you grow and scale, is another way to invest in your business and when done properly can immediately multiply your income. Although we like to bring in friends and family to help us in the early stages of building our business, the best help requires money in return for skill and time. Investing into key performers and efficient consultants also helps with the bottom line and money from the business can be redirected to increase spend in these areas.

Marketing

Marketing is another fantastic way to utilize reinvested dollars. In order to make more money and have longevity inside of your entrepreneur-owned business, you must promote it. Even if you do not have a large budget for marketing, it is a priority piece and deserves to be higher on the list when examining forward financial allocation. If you put money into your business, behind products/services that you know from examination will grow your income, you move into an expansive scaling phase. Great returns come from knowing how to manage your money. Make sure you learn how to and start reinvesting.

How to pull off a below-the-line-campaigns

An advertisement strategy concept designed for businesses to promote their products or services in an unconventional way with little budget to spend. This involved high energy and imagination focusing on grasping the attention of the public on a more personal and memorable level. Some large companies used unconventional advertisement techniques, proclaiming to be guerilla marketing but those companies will have a larger budget and the brand is already visible. The main point of guerilla marketing is that the activities are done exclusively on the streets or other public spaces, such as shopping centers, parks, or beaches a with maximum people so as to attract a bigger audience.

GUERRILLA MARKETING

- VIRAL MARKETING
  - PASSING ON A MESSAGE
  - ENTERTAINING CONTENT

- AMBIENT MARKETING
  - BRAND RECOGNITION
  - SOFT-TELL APPROACH

- AMBUSH MARKETING
  - TAKING OVER EVENTS
  - RIDING WITH HYPE

- EXPERIMENTAL MARKETING
  - INTERACTIVE MARKETING
  - TRIAL PERIODS

Hiring A Marketing Manager

PROS

-Better brand presence online

-More cohesive brand image

-Attracts user to website and products

-Appeals to a larger demographic

CONS

-Not within the budget

-Requires resources and updates regularly

-Might affect professional online presence

-Time-consuming task

Hiring process
for Recruitment purposes

01
Create role openings and share the information

02
Enter applicant data

03
Screen applicants for interviews and assessment

04
Make offers to successful applicants

05
Create role openings and share the information

SEO-STRAT-EGY

Search engine optimisation (SEO) is the process of affecting the visibility of a website or a web page in a web search engine's unpaid results – often referred to as "natural", "organic" or "earned" results. In general, the earlier (or higher ranked on the search result page), and the more frequently a site appears in the search results list, the more visitors it will receive from the search engine's users, and these visitors can be converted into customers. SEO may target different kinds of search, including image search, local search, video search, academic search, news search and industry-specific vertical search engines.

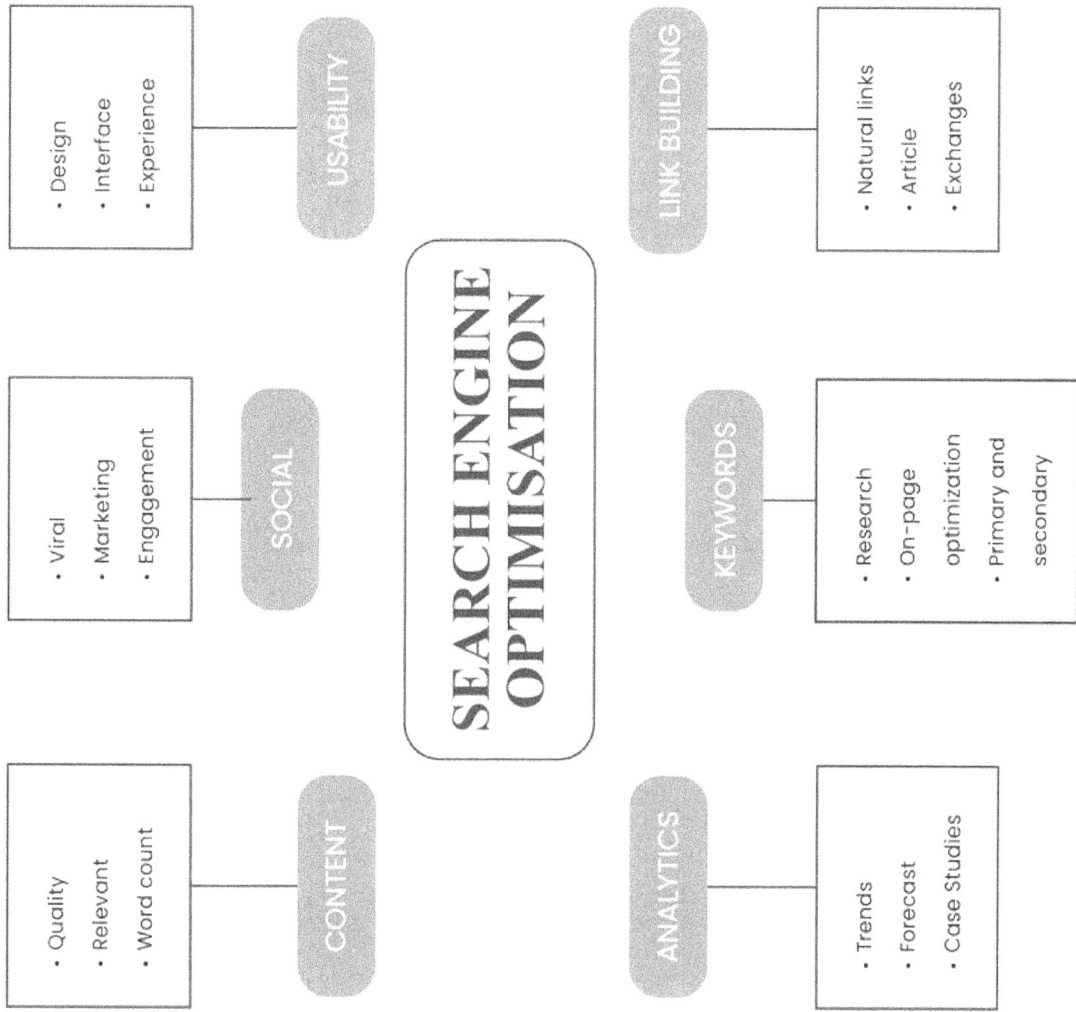

USABILITY
- Design
- Interface
- Experience

SOCIAL
- Viral
- Marketing
- Engagement

CONTENT
- Quality
- Relevant
- Word count

SEARCH ENGINE OPTIMISATION

LINK BUILDING
- Natural links
- Article
- Exchanges

KEYWORDS
- Research
- On-page optimization
- Primary and secondary

ANALYTICS
- Trends
- Forecast
- Case Studies

NOTES

NOTES

NOTES

NOTES

NOTES

10

Passive Income

In *Money Management & Entrepreneurs,* I outline the strategies that I utilize with clients in helping them build very successful businesses. I first, however, used these techniques when starting my business several years ago. After falling on the ground, crying and threatening to quit, I realized I had become a master…an expert on how to go from nothing to something beautiful. Now I am giving these tips to you, in hopes that you too can continue to create something beautiful. So, without further delay, Passive Income.

One of the greatest ways to build wealth, according to the wealthy, is through entrepreneurship—becoming an innovator in your field. Yet once your business has allowed you to accumulate a certain level of wealth, you then get the opportunity to move from active to passive income. Learning to have money that works for you is the goal. Uncovering how to yield higher returns is the journey.

Real estate, stocks, bonds, government equity, etc. all require both knowledge and passion. Note, however, that stocks have the potential to yield a much faster return than bonds or CDs. Conversely, real estate investing involves a different level of knowledge than trading. If trading or real estate investing is not something you plan to take on, research other appreciable opportunities (gold, art, certain types of jewelry, land, businesses, etc...) and stay away from products that depreciate.

Building More Products

Build or create products that people can buy without you being there. Offer services that employees can manage and fulfill. Several of my books are offered on online via Amazon, Barnes and Noble, Walmart, and Kindle, allowing me to make money while I am sleeping. I also offer books at different physical locations around the country. This arrangement requires that the owner of the location receive a percentage of book sales.

Digital products, books and courses are also great examples of goods that can be dropped off, shipped or created to increase passive revenue sales. As of 2019, $450,000 was being spent per day on online education. Create a product, market it, and build passive income. Whatever method you choose to build additional income, position yourself to own the table and hire others to sit there.

Multiple Businesses

Creating multiple businesses or learning to purchase established businesses is another way to create additional/passive income. Note that it is much easier, however, to move faster in revenue creation if the businesses you add to your portfolio, are businesses that are related to your current level of expertise. According to the author of Good to Great, Jim Collins, great companies like Walgreens, Wells Fargo, Gillette, Pitney Bowes and Fannie Mae, do only what fits into their concept.

How to Start

Many years ago, when I started investing, I started investing with $25 a month in my 20s. By my 30s I had over ten thousand dollars invested and was able to put a down payment on my first home and start my first business. I grew in amount of investment and knowledge of how to invest over the years to where I had something that was very useful when I needed it. Getting started is more important than how much you have to start. Secure the knowledgeable you need to be the right type of investor and position yourself to be liquid…very liquid.

GREATNESS MAP

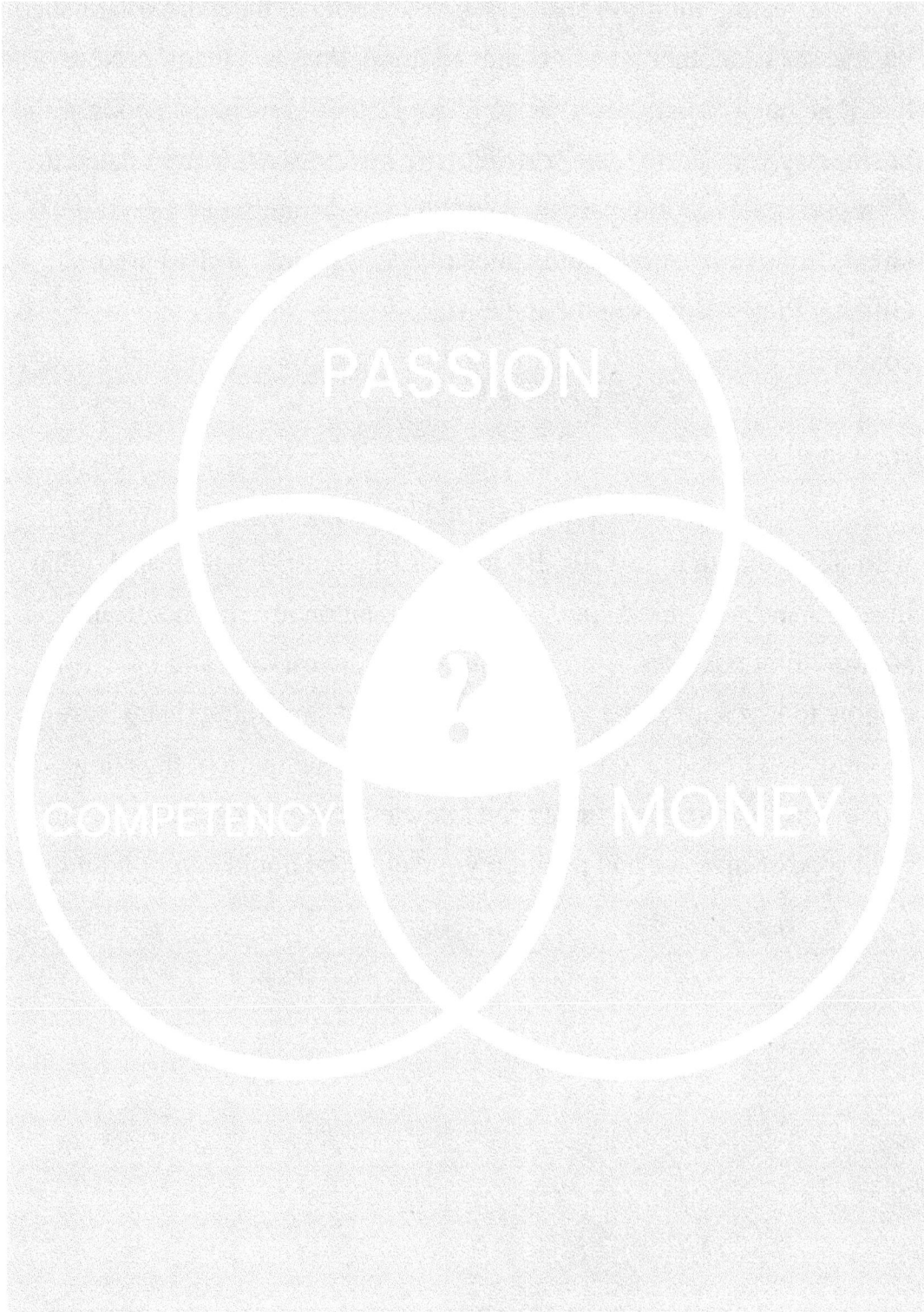

What can i be great at?

1

2

3

4

5

6

7

8

9

10

NOTES

NOTES

NOTES

NOTES

NOTES

Month:_____

SUNDAY	MONDAY	TUESDAY	WEDNESDAY

THURSDAY	FRIDAY	SATURDAY	NOTES

Month: _____

SUNDAY	MONDAY	TUESDAY	WEDNESDAY

THURSDAY	FRIDAY	SATURDAY	NOTES

Month:_____

SUNDAY	MONDAY	TUESDAY	WEDNESDAY

THURSDAY	FRIDAY	SATURDAY	NOTES

Month:_____

SUNDAY	MONDAY	TUESDAY	WEDNESDAY

THURSDAY	FRIDAY	SATURDAY	NOTES

Month:_____

SUNDAY	MONDAY	TUESDAY	WEDNESDAY

THURSDAY	FRIDAY	SATURDAY	NOTES

Month: _____

SUNDAY	MONDAY	TUESDAY	WEDNESDAY

THURSDAY	FRIDAY	SATURDAY	NOTES

Month: _____

SUNDAY	MONDAY	TUESDAY	WEDNESDAY

THURSDAY	FRIDAY	SATURDAY	NOTES

Month:_____

SUNDAY	MONDAY	TUESDAY	WEDNESDAY

THURSDAY	FRIDAY	SATURDAY	NOTES

Month:_____

SUNDAY	MONDAY	TUESDAY	WEDNESDAY

THURSDAY	FRIDAY	SATURDAY	NOTES

Month:_____

SUNDAY	MONDAY	TUESDAY	WEDNESDAY

THURSDAY	FRIDAY	SATURDAY	NOTES

Month:_____

SUNDAY	MONDAY	TUESDAY	WEDNESDAY

THURSDAY	FRIDAY	SATURDAY	NOTES

Month:_____

SUNDAY	MONDAY	TUESDAY	WEDNESDAY

THURSDAY	FRIDAY	SATURDAY	NOTES

Conclusion

When I started my business several years ago, I had $10,000 to invest in the startup. This is money that I had saved over years of working for other people and doing side jobs. The saved funds allowed me to buy the products I needed, it allowed me to position myself in the market, and allowed me to bring on who I needed to bring on to help me grow my business. I also made a lot of mistakes with the money, but I learned valuable tips on what works and how to grow a business. I took a leap into entrepreneurship and I never looked back.

www.ingramcontent.com/pod-product-compliance
Lightning Source LLC
Chambersburg PA
CBHW081534220326

41598CB00036B/6428